RANDALL W. ARK

THE AUTOBIOGRAPHY OF
RANDALL W. ARK

DEEDS PUBLISHING | ATLANTA

Published by Deeds Publishing in Athens, GA
www.deedspublishing.com

Printed in The United States of America

Cover and interior design by Deeds Publishing

ISBN 978-1-961505-45-2

Books are available in quantity for promotional or premium use. For information, email info@deedspublishing.com.

First Edition, 2025

10 9 8 7 6 5 4 3 2 1

I was born at City Hospital (later called Community Hospital) in Springfield, Ohio. My arrival time was 3:05 a.m. on June 2, 1948. My father remarked, "That's the ugliest baby I have ever seen," or so said my mother. Thus began my journey through life.

I had an older brother, Stephen, at the time, who had arrived on January 11, 1947.

My mother recalls that I had a "very good disposition

and was not fussy at all," and when I was three years old, my mother said that whenever we happened to be driving around, I could name nearly every make and model of car I saw on the road. I loved cars, especially the varied tail lights. It was easier to tell cars apart in those days.

By the time I had turned three, another brother, Nicholas, had arrived, on the 28th of July, 1949. After two more brothers and a sister, my sibling family was complete. Mom always said that she was hoping to have twelve children, but a doctor advised her to stop. I now had five siblings. My sister, Nora, was born on my 5th birthday and I always remarked that she was "my sister the most."

I was reared on a small farm that contained a variety of animals: chickens, beef cows, dairy cows, pigs (sows and feeder pigs), and sheep. Oh, and cats and dogs. My mother canned vegetables and fruit and Dad and Grandpa butchered for meat. My Grandma Effie, my father's mother, died in 1949, so I did not get to know her. My Dad said that when she was dying and bedridden, she spoke in German, and it sounded like she was addressing field hands.

My family's farm had a smokehouse, an outhouse, a milk separator on the back porch, a corn grinder, two tractors, a corn elevator, a hay fork that took hay into the upper part of the barn, a two bottom plow, two row corn plows, a hay mower, a hay wagon, a disc, a grain drill, a hay rake, a two row corn planter, and a garden tractor, a trailer, and a one row corn picker. Since our corn picker was not mounted so it could open up a field, we boys had to pick the two outside rows of corn and throw the ears of corn into a trailer as we went clear around the field. I can't say that I ever looked forward to that.

My memories of my Grandpa Ark are sketchy, but it seems like he often wore bib overalls and a straw hat. He also wore suspenders quite a bit. There were occasions when he would come home from town with some maple leaf candy that he bought to share with us kids. It was so sweet, but very good. It was shaped like a maple leaf, too. He also used to chew Blackjack chewing gum, which I never cared for. And he would eat limburger cheese on crackers, which to me smelled like poop! Well, it did!

John J. Ark
Wilbur Ark's father

Above: Grandpa John Ark and older brother, Steve, on the tractor.

My grandpa and my father owned three guns and a pistol. Two shotguns (a 12-gauge shotgun and a .410 shotgun), a .22 rifle, and a small .22 pistol. Occasionally, a possum would make its way into our hen house and get one of our chickens, so they were not welcome on our farm. Well, grandpa found a possum one time, "playing possum," right at the edge of our cornfield in the back of our house. Grandpa said we could take turns shooting that possum. Steve, Nick, and I took turns and shot each gun. The 12-gauge about knocked my shoulder out of joint, I sure remember that. Unfortunately, there were little baby possums just lying there and grandpa stepped on each one to kill them. I didn't care to see that and to this day I can still recall it.

Dad tried to take us hunting once in the back cornfield, but we brothers were not into hunting and killing animals. My dad didn't mind killing snakes, he hated snakes, like Indiana Jones! Regardless, I was around a lot of farm activity growing up.

It wasn't very easy working on our farm. Most of our farm implements and machinery were originally horse drawn, so there were seats attached to many of them. Our plow had a seat, our hay mower had a seat, our disc had a seat, you get the picture.

I lived with three of my siblings (Steve, Nick, and Bruce) in our farmhouse until 1953, which happens to be the year that my big brother, Steve, began first grade at Oak Grove Elementary.

My father had started building another house on our

land, separate from our farmhouse, at the head of our lane that emptied onto Rebert Pike. It was where we lived from 1953 to 1961. It was then that we moved back into the farmhouse. Dad stopped construction on the little house before it was finished and made what was to be a garage into our home.

Stephen, Nick, Bruce, and I slept on two sets of bunk beds in the same area of our house that also served as our dining area. Dad made us boys a closet of sorts, a place to hang our clothes and drawers to put clothes and "stuff" in. My sister Nora and brother, Danny, slept in my parent's bedroom.

Eight people in that little house! Is it any wonder we remain close to this day? As I stated earlier, in 1953, my older brother, Stephen, began his scholastic career at Oak Grove Elementary, situated on the corner of Tecumseh Road and Fairfield Pike.

My father, although he loved farming, began attending school at a Barber College in Columbus and became a licensed barber in 1953. After getting his license to cut hair, he went to work for my Grandpa Gilbert Shump, on Third Street in Dayton. I believe that area was called Drexel, and it wasn't the best area of Dayton. Grandpa Shump was my mother's father. Dad practiced cutting hair by giving us haircuts at home, specializing in burrs and flat-tops.

My great-grandparents, John and Josephine Scurlock, lived for a time with Grandma and Grandpa Shump in Dayton. And when Grandma and Grandpa Scurlock lived in Cedarville, my mother lived with them while attending

Cedarville College. I still, to this day, can't get over the fact that Grandpa Scurlock was 10 years old when Custer fought at the Battle of the Little Big Horn in 1876 and that was also the year that Wild Bill Hickok was shot and killed in Deadwood, South Dakota. Ten years old!!!

John W. and Josephine Scurlock

There was a Mial Scurlock who died at the Alamo in 1836 and a "Doc" Scurlock who rode with Billy the Kid during the Lincoln County Range Wars.

Josiah Gordon "Doc" Scurlock (January 11, 1849 – July 25, 1929) was an American Old West figure, cowboy, and gunfighter. A founding member of the Regulators during the Lincoln County War in New Mexico, Scurlock rode alongside such men as Billy the Kid.

Early life [edit]

He was born in Tallapoosa County, Alabama, January 11, 1849, the sixth of 11 children born to Priestly Norman Scurlock (July 3, 1806 – June 22, 1876) and Esther Ann Brown (May 19, 1819 – June 1, 1903). Josiah was said to have studied medicine in New Orleans, thus receiving his nickname "Doc".

Described as 5 feet 8 inches (1.73 m) tall, weighing 150 pounds (68 kg), with brown eyes and dark blond hair, Doc went to Mexico in about 1870. While there, he and another man had an argument over a card game and drew their pistols. The other man shot first and the bullet went through Doc's mouth, knocking out his front teeth and coming out the back of his neck without any more serious damage. He quickly returned fire and killed the man who shot him.

NATHAN, KARA, MATTHEW: YOUR GREAT-GREAT GRANDPARENTS WERE JOHN AND JOSEPHINE SCURLOCK.

Doc Scurlock

Doc Scurlock, circa 1877

Born	January 11, 1849
	Tallapoosa County, Alabama, USA
Died	July 25, 1929 (aged 80)
	Eastland, Texas, USA
Resting place	Eastland City Cemetery
Nationality	American
Occupation(s)	Gunman, outlaw, cowboy, vigilante
Known for	Lincoln County Regulators

> REMEMBER > BATTLE AND REVOLUTION > DEFENDERS > SCURLOCK, MIAL

BACK TO DEFENDERS

Scurlock, Mial

Age: 26
Rank: Garrison Member
From: North Carolina

Mial Scurlock, Alamo defender, son of Joseph and Martha Jones (Glasgow) Scurlock, was born in Chatham County, North Carolina, on May 25, 1809. He lived for a time in Tennessee and Mississippi. In 1834 he and his brother William took their slaves through Louisiana to Texas and settled in San Augustine. Scurlock volunteered for service in the Texas army on October 17, 1835, and took part in the siege of Bexar. He subsequently served in the Alamo garrison and died in the battle of the Alamo on March 6, 1836.

ROES OF THE ALAMO

ES NOWLAN
ENGLAND

RCE PAGAN
SSISSIPPI

OPHER PARKER
ISSISSIPPI

IAM PARKS
TEXAS

ROSON PERRY
TEXAS

OS POLLARD
SSACHUSETTS

URDY REYNOLDS
NNSYLVANIA

AC ROBINSON
SCOTLAND

THOMAS H. ROBERTS

JAMES ROBERTSON
TENNESSEE

JAMES M. ROSE
OHIO

JACKSON J. RUSK
IRELAND

JOSEPH RUTHERFORD
KENTUCKY

ISAAC RYAN
LOUISIANA

MIAL SCURLOCK
LOUISIANA

MARCUS L. SEWELL
ENGLAND

1836

Mial Scurlock is related to the Ark's
Issac Ryan is related to Don Christian

Good friend Don Christian at The Alamo.
Don also has a relative who served at The Alamo, Isaac Ryan.

Grandpa Ark died in 1958 when I was ten years old. One memory of Grandpa Ark is of him giving us money to fetch the daily newspaper for him from the mailbox at the end of our lane.

After grandpa died, my father began working on the farmhouse down the lane where we (Steve, Nicky, Bruce, and I) began as kids. We moved back into the farmhouse in 1961 after three years of working with Dad putting in central heating, plumbing, adding a bathroom, tearing plaster off the walls, and replacing the walls with drywall, and installing light fixtures. The most amazing project I remember was when Dad lifted the farmhouse with screw jacks in order to lay plastic underneath the house and pour a cement foundation. The farmhouse rested on stones originally.

Remodeling again, years later. My dad working with two of my brothers and two nephews.

My brother Steve's best guess on the age of our farmhouse is probably pre-Civil War or right at the beginning of the war, roughly 150 years ago. Casper Ark was my great-grandfather on my father's side, who came over to America from Germany.

My Aunt Helen, my father's sister, told me that she did

not speak English, only German, until she entered the first grade at Oak Grove.

We kids had to walk up the lane from the farmhouse each morning to "catch the bus." Sometimes, we were a little late getting started up the lane and had to run to get to the bus on time. And some mornings were pretty cold and snowy, but we did it without complaint, mostly. Our bus driver was "Shorty" Gledale. Mom would make him chocolate chip cookies at Christmas.

One of my best friends was Charles D. Swaney. I knew Charlie even before the first grade because our families both attended the same church at Rocky Point Chapel on Old Mill Road. This was over 71 years ago.

Charlie's family lived on Enon Cross Roads (now,

Rocky Point Road) and where they lived was such a great place to explore and play, it was like Clifton Gorge in Yellow Springs. There were rocks to climb, streams to cross, hanging vines to swing on, and caves to explore. We played there often and even camped overnight one time under a cliff overhang. Charlie's mother, Edna, made the best chocolate chip cookies and gingerbread men! And our whole family really enjoyed sledding over at Swaney's in the winter. Charlie is a very successful lawyer, and we remain friends to this day.

Here's some things I remember about attending Rocky Point Chapel on Old Mill Road.

Rocky Point Chapel

Another close friend I had at Rocky Point was Kenny Randall. He had a lot of brothers, like I did. Now, back when we were kids, Rocky Point had a coal oil stove at the rear of the sanctuary and sometimes, Kenny and I would sit back next to the stove where it was warm. No central heating back then. Either it was Kenny or me, I forget who, reached up and turned the knob that turns the heat up. Before long, it was becoming uncomfortably warm in the sanctuary and one of the elders, probably Mr. Southward, came back to where Kenny and I were sitting, and he saw that the knob had been turned up. He turned the knob to where it was supposed to be and said, "You two quit horsing around back here." We did.

One time I was sitting next to Charlie Swaney in church with his family, and I must have said something funny to him that made him laugh out loud, a hearty guffaw. Mrs. Jenny Sparrow was sitting behind us, and she reached up and knuckled Charlie in the back of the head. I wonder if Charlie remembers that.

The kids in the church all took their turns at being acolytes on Sunday morning and were charged with lighting the candles in the front of the church before the service and then putting them out at the close of the service. You couldn't have the shakes if you were an acolyte.

Another duty we performed as kids was passing around the collection plates to collect money to pay the pastor and the church bills. Charley's father, Jack Swaney, (who was 6'5" tall), was the church treasurer and served in that capacity for many years. I remember once when mom put more money in the plate than she had intended, so she took out some money to make up for the large bill she had placed into the plate.

Our church had a nice youth group program, and we were joined with the older youth and everybody got along well. While attending youth group, The Beach Boys came out with the song, "I Get Around" which I loved, and the Supremes had their first big hit, "Baby Love." Sherry Southward loved this song and sang it over and over.

Rocky Point Chapel

Pastor Ed Winkler, Ron Randall, Delbert Grube, Steve Demmy, Lloyd Descombes, David Southward, Larry Grube
Don Randall, ?, Sue Southward, Marabel Rotruck, Sue Descombes, Barbara Rotruck, Russell Randall

We were very naïve kids and one Sunday at youth group, one of the kids brought in a Ouija Board to mess around with. Good grief! Sherry Southward, who was part of our youth group, was a lively girl, and sometimes she would call other kids "buzzard bait." She was fun to be around. She was a younger sister to Sue and David Southward, and had a younger brother, Mike.

Some of the adults at church had the coolest cars. The Randall's had a brand new red and white '59 Chevy Impala, and the Rohrer's had a 1958 robin-egg blue Chevy Impala with a white convertible top. Very cool looking cars.

Each year the church hosted a large outdoor picnic which all the families at church enjoyed. My mother told me that one of the things I liked to do at the picnic was to sit in the circle with the older men and listen to them talk. The older youth played volleyball, but I didn't care to do that. Thanks to my brother, Steve, my wife Sharon and I have one of the pews from Rocky Point that we now use in our home.

For Sunday morning church, all of us boys each wore a certain color sport coat that mom got for us, same pattern, but different colors, a white shirt with cuff links, and a tie with a double Windsor knot or a bow tie, dress pants, and shoes that we had shined the night before. My sister always wore a nice, little girl's dress.

I remember that if you came to church every Sunday for a whole year without missing, you earned a little attendance pin. As the years go by and you obtained more attendance pins, you could chain them together to hang down and everyone could see all the years you had perfect attendance. It was kind of like a status symbol. The longest ones I remember seeing were worn on Elenore Taylor and Jenny Sparrow's coats.

I did not attend kindergarten but started first grade in 1954 at Oak Grove Elementary located where Tecumseh Road crosses Fairfield Pike. I learned that my father had also attended Oak Grove back when it was a high school, years before.

Oak Grove High School
Open in 1921

I established many friendships in the first grade, and some would continue through high school and beyond. And the older I get, the more fortunate I feel that I had so many good friends to share my life with. Many remain alive today, aging into their mid-70's. The names of some of those friends were Sandra Shank, Roger Clem, Sally Parks, Jackie Workman, Kay Holsapple, Fred Henry, Scott Elliot and Christine Yeazell. My first-grade teacher in 1954 at Oak Grove was Miss Gordon and the principal was Mr. Laird.

1954 - 1955

Miss Gordon was heavyset, and I reasoned at the time that the bigger you were, the older you must be, because you've had more time to eat. One day, at recess, I asked Miss Gordon how old she was, and she replied, "How old do you think I am?" I replied, "Oh, about a hundred." She laughed and said, "Not quite."

Classmate Sandy Shank was hard-pressed to keep from talking in class, and one time Miss Gordon had Sandy come to the front of the class and sit in her big wooden chair that she used when she read to the class. Miss Gordon then walked over and sat on top of Sandy and Sandy disappeared behind the body of Miss Gordon. We laugh about this to this day. Miss Gordon also sat on Jackie Workman now and then.

Sandy Shank & Jack Workman

I found out very recently from classmate, Sally Parks, that one time when we first grade students were coming into Miss Gordon's class after recess, my friend, Charlie Swaney, was holding the door open while we all were entering the classroom. Sally told me that as she walked by, Charlie bent forward and kissed her on the cheek. I asked Charlie about this event to get a verification, and he said that Miss Gordon grabbed him by the shoulders and shook him really good! I couldn't help but laugh, but I was amazed that I had never heard this tale before, and I'm 76 years old.

It was also in the first grade that Sally Parks, had a birthday party at her house on Hagen Rd. Sally's birthday was celebrated on the 4th of July, so as a younger child she assumed that all the celebrations and festivities were for her. A logical assumption, I think.

I absolutely loved going to parties back then. Sally's father, George Parks, was our family's milkman for a few years.

George Parks

The thing that really captured my attention at that party was a TV set in their living room. I had never seen one before and I was totally mesmerized, and it wasn't even turned on! The screen was small and round, and my gaze was transfixed on that mysterious piece of furniture. My parents would not purchase a TV set until I was in the second grade, which was about 1955.

Compared to today's TV's, our family's TV was about as rudimentary as it gets. It had very limited reception (channels 2, 7, maybe 10) and the black and white picture was not only *not* high definition, but you also felt like you had suddenly developed cataracts in both eyes while watching it. Regardless, my siblings and I thought it was wonderful to have a TV.

Some of our favorite shows back then were *Lassie, Rin Tin Tin, Fury, Superman, Mickey Mouse Club, the Wonderful World of Disney, Zorro, Gunsmoke, Have Gun Will Travel, Red Skelton, Roy Rogers, The Lone Ranger, Captain Kangaroo, Mighty Mouse, Twilight Zone,* and many more, mostly westerns. My good friend Roger Clem loved watching *The Three Stooges* and he would tell us all about it at school, but we didn't get that channel. Here it is, 2024, and my grandsons like watching *The Three Stooges.*

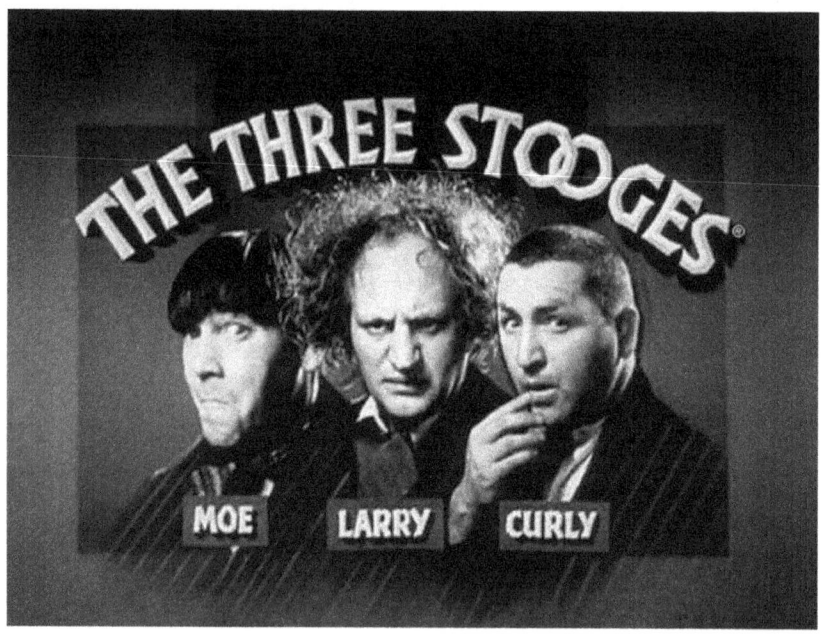

Watching Walt Disney programs were not only entertaining, but they were educational. I learned how to spell e-n-c-y-c-l-o-p-e-d-i-a from Jiminy Cricket and I loved the lessons I learned when Jiminy Cricket sang the lyrics to "I'm no fool, no siree, I want to live to be ninety-three, I play it safe for you and me, cause I'm no fool."

Some favorite shows I remember were *Spin and Marty, Applegate's Treasure, Davy Crockett, Texas John Slaughter, Elfego Baca, Corky and White Shadow, the Dirango Dude, the Mark of Zorro, Ichabod Crane, Brer Fox and Brer Rabbit,*

Pecos Bill, and many more. Good clean entertainment and usually presented with a moral.

My mother came to observe class one day when I was in the first grade. We were having addition math drills and races on the chalk board. I remember racing against Chuck Burgess, and I missed the problem 5+3. I felt embarrassed, mainly because my mother was there. I have never forgotten from then on, that 5+3=7... wait, what?

There were many ways a kid might get hurt at recess back then at Oak Grove, and some of the playground equipment was downright deadly or we strived to make it deadly. Classmate Woody Holmes was accidently hit in the head with a baseball bat one time and needed stitches, Sherry Boggs fell from the monkey bars and broke her arm, and after that, the school lowered the monkey bars so much so that our feet dragged on the ground trying to cross the monkey bars. Thanks, Sherry.

We used to swing as high as we could and then bail out onto the ground, and our two-story metal slides created a g-force on the way down

But I think the most dangerous piece of equipment on the playground, however, was our merry-go-round.

The seats were made of splintered wood and the whole unit was low to the ground. One or two students would start pushing the merry-go-round, running as fast as they could, hoping someone would fly off. A more dangerous way to get the merry-go-round going was to get in the middle part and push from that vantage point. Heaven help you if you happen to trip and fall while pushing from the middle. Students took their lives in their own hands to ride the merry-go-round!

There was a girl student at Oak Grove who was a couple of years ahead of me and who was very short, wore braces on her arms and legs, and walked with crutches. Her name was Mickey. She had been stricken with polio, the same as President Franklin D. Roosevelt. Getting polio was a scary thing in the 1950's.

Every student in the school had to be vaccinated each year with a polio vaccine in the 1950's. In the beginning, the vaccine was given as a shot, then, a liquid vaccine came along, thank goodness. And about everyone back then was sporting a round scar on one of their shoulders that was left by a smallpox vaccine injection. I remember that large scab it left on my arm after first getting the vaccination.

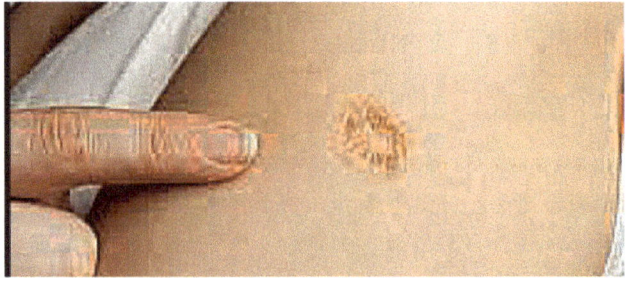

I would often see the older boys playing marbles at recess. My father made each of us kids a small leather bag to carry our marbles in. Now, the bigger marbles were called "boulders," and there were lead and metal marbles called "steelies." There were "cat's eye" marbles and clear and colored "crystal marbles."

To this day, I have yet to figure this one out. One day there were some older boys playing marbles in the hard dirt because it was a smoother surface to shoot marbles on. My friend, Charlie, along with me, was standing there watching some older boys play, and all of a sudden he places his foot over Phil Brown's marbles and pushes them down into the hard-packed earth. Phil Brown was a known bully and not to be messed with. Why in heaven's name would Charlie do that, did he have a death wish?

Well, Phil started to get up and Charley took off running. Luckily. Charlie was a pretty fast runner for his age, and he could run for a long time, a skill which served him well in high school track.

I asked Charlie about this event. This is what he told me, "*He chased me around the Oak Grove School building a couple times before I ran into our schoolroom and into the cloakroom; he came right in after me, and when Mrs. Owens (or Mrs. Graham, I can't remember who) heard the story, they made me apologize to Phil.*"

"But Charlie," I asked, "What in tarnation made you

do such a foolish thing?" He responded, "A brief flash of bravery/stupidity when someone dared me to do it (don't remember who, but it is the kind of thing I could easily attribute to Jack Workman)." I agreed, Jackie would be a likely candidate to dare Charlie.

Charlie Swaney and Jackie Workman

I stayed overnight at Jackie's house once, and I remember sword fighting in an upstairs room with a couple of swords that his father brought back from Japan in WWII. Yes, it was a dumb thing to do, since the swords were real. I still remember the sound of cold steel clanging as we parried each other's attempts to impale each other (not really). We then decided to create a train track using every length of track that Jackie had. We set up the track so that the track would end, and the train would go out the upstairs window, and fall to the ground from two stories up. We called it the "Train of Death!"

My second and third grade teacher was Mrs. Owens. She was a very nice teacher, and she had three children that we were all friends with: Faith, Sonja, and Billy.

Mrs. Owens

Mrs. Graham was my teacher in the 4th grade. She was sometimes handy with a board paddle when she needed to be, but she was a very good and dedicated teacher. She and her husband, Mr. Frank Graham, both attended our country church in the wildwood, Rocky Point Chapel. Mr. Graham also taught my father as a student at Oak Grove when the school served as a high school.

Mrs. Betty Graham 4th

Mrs. Graham had a substitute one day and Jackie Workman and I had tracked mud into the classroom from outside recess and our good friend, Charlie, thought it was his duty to tell on us.

Well, the substitute teacher stood Jackie and me up in front of the class and asked the class if we should be paddled for tracking in mud and they all screamed, "YES!," that we should be paddled. I could feel the love. Jackie and I were given three cracks each with a board paddle and sent to the restroom to clean off our shoes. I think we shunned Charlie for a whole recess after that.

Later in life when Mrs. Graham was dying, and in the hospital bedridden, I went to see her and we talked and reminisced and she stopped talking suddenly and then said, "You know I loved all you boys."

I can't remember what grade it was when I started getting books to read from the bookmobile that frequented our school. I know that Charlie, Roger, and I loved to read a certain genre of book available on the bookmobile. We devoured books that were biographies of historic Americans like George Washington Carver, Thomas Edison,

Davy Crockett, Daniel Boone, Abraham Lincoln, Ulysses S. Grant, Thomas Jefferson, George Washington, Alexander Graham Bell, and the Wright Brothers.

There was something else that happened in the fourth grade that had an affect on me. One day, one of the students remarked that there was a fire a few fields over to the north of Oak Grove. Our classroom was partially underground, so it was all we could do to see anything out the window at ground level. This was in Mrs. Graham's class.

We later found out that it was Mr. Sayre Jenkins' house that had caught fire and nearly burned to the ground. Sayre was a widowed man who farmed when he could. He had very old farm equipment, mostly antique. Well, Sayre fixed himself a place to live in his cowbarn and that's where he lived out his days. He never rebuilt his home. He was a regular attendee at our Rocky Point Church also.

When I was in high school, I bought a Hereford steer from Sayre to raise as an FFA project. I named my steer Mushy, which I now think was a very stupid name. My friend, Charles Swaney, helped Sayre in the summer with farm work.

Charles Swaney, son of Mr. and Mrs. Jack Swaney, Springfield, Route 1, shocks wheat on the farm of Sayre Jenkins on the Rebert pike near Greenon High School. The experience is one that few boys his age in this area will encounter. The binding and threshing of wheat is a harvesting method that has been in rare use since World War II. Mr. Jenkins has not abandoned the binder in favor of the more modern combine and says that he plans to continue its use.

I don't mean to leave out teachers, Miss Shaw and Mrs. Pallant, as elementary teachers, but I can't remember anything special happening under their tutelage, at least not to me.

When I was in the sixth grade, my teacher was Mr. A.A. Arthur. He was a real stickler for holding your pencil or pen just right when writing, and he would walk up and down the desk isles with a ruler and smack your knuckles if you were not holding your pencil correctly. It didn't matter if your writing resembled hieroglyphics, as long as you held your pencil as he instructed.

45 Years of teaching…

I forget what day of the week it was, but it seems I remember we had a "milk day" where everyone would be given a little glass bottle of milk.

Since I always tried to mimic whatever Charlie did, he and I were the only ones in the entire class to get white milk, everyone else got chocolate. I wanted shoes like Charlie's, a yellow corduroy shirt like Charlie's, a fringe leather jacket like Charlie's. And it always seemed like Charlie had patches sewn onto his jeans where the knees were. Instead of having to buy new jeans, many parents just sewed on patches. Being in "style" did not exist at Oak Grove. Well, maybe it did for girls. Another thing that most parents did back then was buy jeans with the pant legs long enough to allow for growth, so we had to cuff them up while we were growing.

Scott Elliott and I became close friends in the 5th and 6th grades. Scott was left-handed, which I thought was pretty cool. His family had two or three horses that we used to ride bareback, which always made me nervous about falling off. Charlie had a horse named Buck, but I was afraid of that horse, because he would sometimes try to bite you.

Scott's father was an Air Force pilot and worked at Wright Patterson Air Force Base. He took Scott and me swimming at the base pool one time and loud music was playing over the intercom. One of the songs they played was "Like A Tiger" by Fabian. I fell in love with that song and eventually bought a 45-rpm record of it.

Another thing that Scott and I did was to stay in at recess when one of our classmates needed help and was struggling with spelling and math.

Scott Elliott

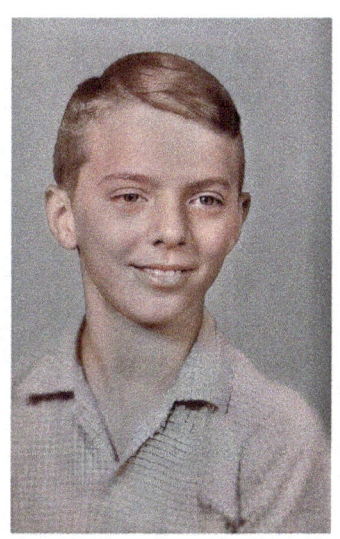

Roger Smith

His name was Roger, a very nice and quiet kid, and Scott and I would help him study. I went to Roger's funeral a couple of years ago and found out that he was stationed very close to me in Vietnam, at Lai Khe, when I was there in 1968-69. I wish I would have known.

My family had a tradition every Saturday night. While watching "*Gunsmoke,*" which was on right after "*Have Gun Will Travel,*" we all were treated to a 5th Avenue candy bar and a small glass of 7-Up. I could make that candy bar last at least 1/2 hour by nibbling down each of the sides, then across the bottom, and lastly, I ate what was left on top, which was the rest of the candy bar with the chocolate covered top and two almonds. We all liked that tradition

If I remember correctly, our allowance was $.25 / week. Sometimes Dad, when he came home from work (barbering), would empty out his pocket of change onto the kitchen table, and we proceeded to divide it up and you better believe, we HAD to be fair about it.

One day, at Oak Grove, I was outside just walking around at recess and a boy named Dennis Ramey was sitting on the steps leading up to Miss Gordon's room. He began speaking with me and he told me he had a paper route and that he made $7.00 a week delivering papers. That was like a million dollars to me. He reached into his pocket and pulled out a quarter and handed it to me. Oh my gosh, that was a week's allowance to me. I was going to save it for the Clark County Fair.

Dennis Ramey

The morning when my family would take us kids to the Clark County Fair, our parents always scheduled dental appointments for each of us with Dr. Shirley K. Schnieder. That never concerned me because I was cavity free, until Vietnam. I forgot to mention that the week before the fair, Mom would sometimes take us into Springfield, usually to the Sears and Roebuck Store, and we would get new jeans and tennis shoes for the upcoming school year.

With all six of us kids packed into the car, we headed to the Clark County Fair after leaving the dentist, sporting our new duds. We kids knew the roads to the fair and kept watch on who would first see the Ferris Wheel in the distance and would chant. "I see the Ferris Wheel; I see the Ferris Wheel!" Poor mom and dad.

I enjoyed seeing all the newest farm equipment on display and shooting arrows with a bow at balloons tied onto bales of hay. I thought I might give the Tilt-a-Whirl a spin (no pun intended) but soon learned that this body of mine was not made for spinning. Upon exiting the ride, I was light-headed and close to vomiting. The Merry-Go-Round was more my speed.

There was this large water faucet positioned near the ceiling of the Mercantile Building. It had a steady stream of water flowing out of it, but the faucet wasn't connected to anything. The water emptied into a wooden tub on the floor and ran continuously. It was truly a mystery to me, and I was fascinated watching it.

But the most vivid memory I have is of a farm safety display, also in the Mercantile Building, where a display depicted a manikin farmer placed in front of a single row corn picker with his leg caught in the rollers of the corn picker header and there was blood everywhere. It was scary, but fascinating at the same time. You just knew that farmer's leg was coming off. That display sure made an impression on me. By living on a farm, you try to be aware of all the possible ways you could get hurt, and there are many. You really had to be careful around certain machinery. Especially machinery that functioned with a power take off.

Mom and Dad usually bought us boys a cowboy hat each at the fair. We loved wearing those hats.

One year mom and dad took us to the Ohio State Fair and Roy Rogers was there, "The King of the Cowboys!" I think my brother, Steve, was able to shake his hand as he rode by in the arena. Roy was a great role model for us kids, for sure. Little did I know it then, that one of my classmates, Linda Spahr, would one day be chosen as the Ohio State Fair Queen, and that my girlfriend at the time, Peggy Shank, would be chosen 2nd runner-up State FFA Queen, and both were Clark County FFA queens.

Summers seemed longer back then. My older brother, Steve, would set up baseball diamonds in our yard to play baseball or wiffle ball. Our neighbors who lived down the road (Rebert Pike and Karen Woods) would come over and we'd choose up sides and play ball. Our teams usually consisted of either Tim Turner, Roger Tillman, Dick Tillman, Paul Rohrer, Chuck Fenwick, Paul Rohrer, or maybe the Dillon twins and Gerry Collingsworth.

I wrote this poem in 1974 to my younger brother, Nick, for his birthday.

"Poem to My Brother" by Randy Ark (1974)

Remember the summers that seemed so long,
We'd wait for the fair and mow the lawn.
Countless innings of playing ball,
Turning leaves at the break of Fall.
Remember the dreams and all those plans,
Life was free with no demands.
The times we shared, as families do,
I remember them well, how about you?

And so as it happened, we grew out of youth,
Straightened our course and pulled our last tooth.
But the best part of all, as the new life begins,
We became more than brothers, we became friends.
Randy Ark

Paul Rohrer, even though three or four years older than I, became close friends and he often looked out for me when I was playing sports with older kids. Many times, on a Saturday morning after a Friday night's football game at Greenon, Paul and I would ride our bikes to the football field and look under the bleachers for money that people might have dropped. Never a substantial haul, but always something, and fun.

Another favorite thing we did as neighborhood kids was to ride our bikes to where Greenon High School was located, and across the road was the Valley Dairy Store on Rebert Pike. It was there we would buy a pack of baseball cards, if we had enough money. I think they were $.05 or $.10 a pack. I didn't care for the bubble gum that came with the pack.

Paul drove a '48 Chevy when old enough to drive. It was black and shiny as I recall.

Paul was the first basketball player I ever witnessed who could dunk a basketball, two-handed, even. He could only do it in warm-ups, though, because players were not allowed to dunk during games back then. And you couldn't hang on the rim like they do these days, it would come down for sure. There were no 3-point lines either. Paul and I remain friends to this day.

Randy Ark and Paul Rohrer
December 4, 2015

Christmas was always fun at our house and something to look forward to. On Christmas Eve, Mom and Dad would get us all in the car and we'd ride into Springfield to look at the Christmas lights. Even though we enjoyed the lights, at the same time we wanted to be sure that we got back home in time for Santa's arrival.

At our church, which was located on Old Mill Road, and was called Rocky Point Chapel and served as a schoolhouse in the past. When it became close to Christmas time, the church always held some sort of get-together in the evening and usually while someone was speaking, we'd hear the sound of sleigh bells ringing outside and our hearts began beating faster because we knew Santa was coming and was close.

We anxiously waited to see if we could see Santa walking by the windows on his way in, and we began to hear him loudly exclaim, "Ho, Ho, Ho!" Santa entered with a bag full of gifts that were supplied by the parents of the kids there. And everyone there received a little cardboard box of Christmas candy.

There is no greater feeling than believing that something is real when you are young, things like Santa Claus and Santa's Elves, the Easter Bunny, and the Tooth Fairy.

Our childhoods were filled with fantastic fantasies, fantasies that made life a wonderland.

On one of our church Christmas gatherings, my father taught me a valuable lesson on compassion and giving. All the gifts had been handed out and I was digging into my candy when my father pulled me aside and said, "There is a little boy over there who didn't get a gift because his parents didn't know to bring one for Santa to give him. I think it would be nice if you gave him your gift and tell him it is from Santa."

In the tapestry of life, parents can see more of the tapestry than children can, but it was difficult for me to give up my gift to some boy I didn't even know. But my father was always doing stuff like this: when looking for a puppy for us kids, he picked the runt of the litter because it probably would never get picked by anyone; when we went to pick out a Christmas tree, he'd suggest a tree that most people would not pick, and we would get that one. That's the kind of man he was. Dad was a good man.

I have fond memories of Christmas morning when Mom and Dad and the six of us kids all lived in the little house at the end of our lane that emptied out onto Rebert Pike. Brothers, Steve, Nicky, Bruce, and I all slept in the same area that also served as our dining room. We slept on two sets of bunk beds. Oh, the conversations we must have had. My brother, Bruce, got it into his head that our skeletons (skelekins) came out of our bodies at night, when we were asleep. Maybe they do, how would I know?

If I recall correctly, we boys didn't sleep too much on Christmas Eve and we diligently watched a special alarm clock that mom placed on the dining table because it had illuminated hands that we could see in the dark.

Typically, it was about 5:00 a.m. when we dared to venture out of our area to see if Santa had come. My brother, Bruce, was usually the one we picked to "test the waters" and see if Santa had come and then try to get mom and dad up and ask if we could open presents. Our parents knew that we would be rising early on Christmas morning, it was a given.

Each year a huge Sears Catalog would come in the mail and we boys and Nora, would look at all the gun and holster sets that we might ask for, for Christmas. Kara would look at the dolls and kitchenettes that were available then.

Since western TV shows occupied a lot of our viewing time on TV, we were all aware of who wore what guns and who had what gear: Roy Rogers, Hop-a-long Cassidy, Gene Autry, The Lone Ranger and Tonto, Have Gun Will Travel, the Fanner 50 pistol, horses for each cowboy, Double RR Bar Ranch set, Fort Apache set complete with Rusty and Rin Tin-Tin. Looking through the Sears catalog was fun to do.

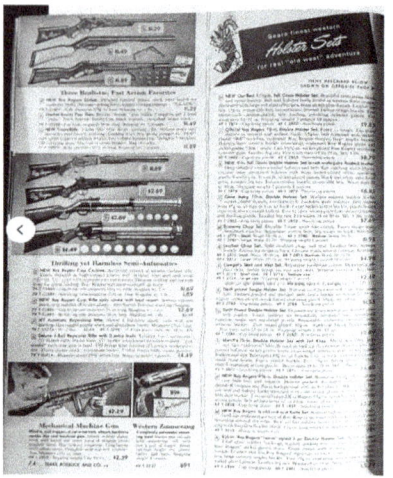

I enjoyed playing with Lincoln Logs, plastic red bricks and building model cars and model airplanes. I enjoyed coloring, tracing, and drawing, too.

I believe it was in the fourth grade, in Mrs. Graham's room, that sometimes she would have a show and tell day where students would bring things in to show the class and tell about what they had brought.

One student brought in his father's .22 pistol and just laid it on his desk waiting for his turn to show it. If that happened today, a SWAT team would soon arrive. When Mrs. Graham saw the pistol, she came to his desk and picked it up and said, "I'll just hold on to this for now." Today, that kid would still be behind bars! But it was 1957 and things were different then.

When I was 11 years old and in the 6th grade, my good friend Jackie Workman sat in front of Mrs. Graham's class and played his guitar. Boy, did he get a lot of attention. I decided then and there that I would ask my parents for a guitar and take lessons. They bought me an acoustic guitar and I took guitar lessons at a music store in the Arcade!

Later on in life, I would be glad that I did. Jackie could play a guitar, Roger Clem could play an accordion, and Charlie Swaney could play a violin, but Charlie did not play in front of the class.

I have to say, ashamedly, that I totally lost it if a student passed gas in the classroom, and it could be heard, especially by me. I began laughing and I could not stop laughing, really *could... not... stop*! I was even made once to go out into the hall and stay there until I could stop laughing. When our principal, Mr. Laird saw me in the hall, I stopped laughing.

I forgot to mention that one time in the fourth grade, when I took off my winter coat to hang it in the cloakroom, I discovered that I only had a white t-shirt on. I had forgotten to put on a regular shirt. So, I asked my good friend, Charlie Swaney, to take his shirt off so I wouldn't be the only one in class wearing only a t-shirt. He did. Begrudgingly. A true friend, indeed.

The Maypole Dance was an event held at the Greenon High School gymnasium. We music students dressed up and our parents came to watch us, sitting in the bleachers.

I think it was at this event that Scott Elliot and I bought corsages for Cheryl Boggs and Cindy Niday. Cindy had invited me to a Job's Daughters Dance previously. Luckily, Chubby Checker's hit record at the time was "The Twist" so, I could easily do that dance. Cindy and I were born on the same day, June 2, 1948, in the same Community Hospital and more than likely we were in the same nursery together. We affectionately refer to each other as twins.

Cheryl Boggs

Cindy Niday

Jill Linkinhoker / Lynne Valentine / Pat Thompson / Jimmy Eldridge / Susan Lambert / Mike Kiley

Christina Shoup

May Day / May Pole Dance

Well, our main event for the evening was to form a circle around an upright pole that had colorful streamers affixed to it, hanging down from the top. Each student was to approach the pole and pick out a streamer with a name card attached to it and take it back to where they were standing in the circle.

The object was when the music began, the students would weave in and out of each other until the pole was colorfully wrapped, looking like Chinese handcuffs, remember those?

Each streamer had a card affixed to it by means of a safety pin. Once the student had retrieved a ribbon, they were to remove the card and keep the safety pin. Before we began our orderly weaving, we began sticking whoever was in front of us in the butt with our pins, which made the person ahead of us lose their concentration and his or her weave was not so orderly. Our music teacher was not amused at all. Our May Pole looked like a typhoon hit it.

On another note, my friend, Charlie, used to crawl out the window at the rear of the room during music class and drop down from the second floor onto a cement dumpster and then onto the ground and then he was free to run around. He somehow crawled back in unnoticed. He was pretty good at it.

One measure of discipline that was used at Oak Grove to keep everyone in line was the rumor that Principal Laird had an "electric paddling machine" in his principal's office. We all had different versions of what this machine looked like and how it functioned. I wonder who started that rumor.

On the last day of school in the sixth grade, Charlie and I rode our bicycles to Oak Grove School to get our report cards and to eat lunch outside. I was always nervous, afraid that I would be held back for some reason, and must repeat a grade, even though my grades were never below a

"B." It was a big fear of mine and to me, a fate worse than death to be held back.

Inside each report card envelope was a Clark County Fair ticket for students to get in free into the Clark County Fair on the Wednesday of fair week.

An added treat for me on the last day, was that mom packed two Hostess Cup Cakes instead of just one.

I have many good memories of my Oak Grove days. Country kids at a country school. Moms packing our lunches and some students had a thermos with something in it, a beverage or maybe soup. We had milk day, library truck day, we gave each other Valentine's Day cards and placed them into boxes that we had fashioned. We had a baseball game against Boone Station, we went to a symphony concert at Memorial Hall and anxiously waited to hear the William Tell Overture, we walked through Ohio Caverns, we said the Pledge of Allegiance every morning, we had show-and-tell day, and more. Good memories.

I finished the sixth grade at Oak Grove Elementary and entered 7th grade at the newly built Hustead Jr. High School located on Hustead Road. This was in 1960. The principal there was Lloyd Monnin and my homeroom teacher was Mr. Larry Hill. Mr. Hill would eventually become the superintendent of our school district. In those days, a person could begin teaching after only two years of college and would finish college while teaching school. Mr. Hill fell into that category. He attended Wittenberg University here in Springfield.

Hustead Elementary School

Hustead Elementary School

3600 Hustead Rd

Hustead School
March 29, 2016

Home of
Randall W. Ark

Directly across the hallway was an 8th grade class, Mr. Kenneth Varner's room. My brother, Steve, was in his room. Now, Mr. Varner's manner kind of scared me, so I kept my distance from him. But he and Mr. Hill seemed to be good friends, and they would visit each other across the hall. I could hear them laughing sometimes in the hallway. I remember Mr. Varner being a very good basketball foul shooter. It was our class that coined the title "Hustead Huskies!" for our school.

One funny thing that happened in the 8th grade was when Mr. Varner gave a math test and a student we called "Kentucky (Kain-tucky)" Craycraft asked another student taking the test, Tom Conley, if he could copy off Tom's test. Tom handed over his test paper to "Kentucky."

Well, the next day, Mr. Varner was getting ready to hand out the math tests and then he asked the class, "Do I have two Tom Conley's in here?" Turn's out that Bill "Kain-Tucky" Craycraft had not only copied Tom's math answers, but also his name! Of course, many of us were thinking, OMG! Bill Craycraft was a good kid, and we all liked him.

Years later, I discovered that Bill Craycraft had his own business here in Springfield, an appliance store located on Selma Rd. I stopped in to see him and we hugged and reminisced about Hustead School and what we had done in our lives. Roger Clem and his wife Peggy happened to be in town one time, and I took them to see Bill. You just can't beat old school friendships. It was so good to see him again.

We all liked Mr. Hill. He seemed interested in what was going on in the world and one day he brought a TV into our classroom on a cart so we students could witness astronaut Alan Sheppard go into space. Alan Bartlett Shepard Jr. was an American astronaut. In 1961, he became the second person and the first American to travel into space, and in 1971, he became the fifth and oldest person to walk on the Moon, at age 47.

My closest friend in the 7th and 8th grades at Hustead Junior High was Jon Allison. We both enjoyed running track. Jon was a natural sprinter and a faster runner than I was, but I tried to keep up. Jon and I were both asked to participate in a local Junior Olympics to be held at South High's Evans Stadium. We both high jumped 5'2" in the 7th grade, using the Western Roll. The 7th grade was also when I became acquainted with Jim Maurer, who later in life would become a very close friend.

Jon Allison

Breakfast at the Melodee in Medway
Randy Ark   Jon Allison

There were some kids who needed to repeat the 7th grade at Enon Jr. High, and they were sent to Hustead to be in our 7th grade. Jim Maurer was one of those students who had come to Hustead from Enon. Jim was very athletic in football and basketball. We were always friends throughout high school, and as I stated before, he and I were to become very close friends just after graduating from high school in 1966. Like many of us, he lived on a farm.

I did not enjoy playing football at the time but decided to go out anyway because many of my friends had. Mr. Dan Winters was our coach. Believe it or not, my helmet did not have a face guard, nothing, nada, not even one bar. Well, on one play at practice, Dick Penewit (was one who came over from Enon) hit my face head-on, headfirst. I was sure my nose was broken. It was big enough already, but now this? Ok, I'd had enough of this football crap. Too much pain. Maybe basketball or track would be more suitable.

Hustead's football team went undefeated in the 8th grade, due mainly to one play, "the Conley pass!" Tom

Conley was a 6'4" red head who, once he caught a pass from our quarterback, it was goodbye granny.

I had never played much basketball up to that point in my life, but I played enough quarters in the 8th grade to earn a varsity letter "H," but it was evident I was not a "natural." I did have a pretty good two hand set shot, though.

I remember listening to Wittenberg's basketball games on the radio and hearing the names Al Thrasher and Bob Cherry quite a bit. More than once did Al Thrasher take the last second shot to win a game. And Bob Cherry was a very gifted athlete and qualified for the Olympics in the high hurdles.

Track and field seemed to be more my forte. High jump, long jump (broad jump), hurdles, sprints, I participated in them all. It was mentioned before about Jon Allison and me both high jumping at Evans Stadium in the Junior Olympics.

So, here I am in 1962 at Greenon High School starting my freshman year. Kinda scary, but exciting, too. You won't believe it, but I went out for football as a freshman. I needed to earn my "66" numerals for my future letter sweater. At one point I think our team usually had 11 players, which meant that each of us played the entire game on offense and defense. One game in particular was during an ice storm. Didn't care for that game.

Roger Clem's position on the team was "center" and I was the "right guard." I depended on Roger to tell me who I was supposed to block on each play.

Now, I had never outdone my brother, Steve, in the high jump, and I never hoped to. Steve was one of Greenon's varsity high jumpers on our track team.

One day, in 1965, as a junior, while competing in Coach Jim Water's Track Decathlon as part of gym class, Steve and I were the last two left in the high jump contest. We were high jumping in Greenon's gym which happened to be full of students coming in from lunch. Everyone was watching. I always seemed to get some kind of boost when performing in front of a crowd. That day was no different.

I high jumped 5'7.5", the highest I had ever jumped in my life, beating my brother by ½". Needless to say, that never happened again… I kind of felt sorry for my big brother, but I was happy to do as well as I did.

For three years, our high school track team was undefeated and went on to win county meets each year. I set a school long jump record of 20' 1" as a sophomore. My coach said my record stood for six years. I set this record when competing against Randy Trostle from Tecumseh High School. He jumped 21'. Oh well… I shouldn't complain though, he qualified for the state track meet.

With a leap of 20'1" Randy Ark sets a new school record for the long jump. He was the first to clear 20' in the school's history.

Senior Jeff Michael gracefully runs the 120 yd. high hurdles

My classmate and good friend, Rod McElwee, set a new high jump record at 6'4.5" using the western roll style and Charles Swaney was nearly unbeatable in the mile and the 1/2 mile races and was unbeaten in the regular track season.

Senior **Rodney McElwee** leaps 6'4 1/2" for a new school record in the high jump.

Our shuttle hurdle relay team of Steve Ark, Bill Jarrel, Mike Schlepp, and Jeff Michael nearly set a state record. Jon Allison and I served as alternates for the team.

SHUTTLE HURDLE	ARK / JARELL MICHAEL / SCHLEPP	59.2	1965

My brother, Steve, was a very good high hurdler. I always liked to watch him race and was very proud of what he could do.

At a special Springfield relay, I remember a sprinter from Dayton Dunbar High School who everybody called

"Peachy Wallace." He was extraordinarily fast and won every race he entered. We were all very impressed with Peachy's speed. He also took home first place ribbons at the State Meet in Columbus, Ohio.

In fact, it turns out that Peachy Wallace won the state track meet by himself.

I recently learned that a good friend of mine, who attended Urbana High School and was a good sprinter in his own right, raced against Peachy Wallace. He lost but was very impressed with Peachy.

Now, varsity letters in track and field were smaller than the varsity football and basketball letters, which really looked cool on a varsity sweater. Well, my ego demanded a "big" varsity letter, but I knew I would never get a varsity letter in basketball, so my plan was to go out for football, again, my senior year, play enough quarters to get a varsity letter, and then lay back and enjoy the rest of the season.

After a while, I began to like playing, so it all worked out. Just as an aside, when I taught Junior High kids, whenever the kids would ask me if I played football in high school, I would tell them, "I sure did."

"What position did you play, Mr. Ark?" I told them that I played "left out."

Track Varsity Letter

My position on the team was right halfback on offense and corner linebacker on defense. Tom Lockwood was my halfback coach and Mr. Jim Waters was our head team coach. I scored a touchdown our very first game on an end run. From then on, I was mostly used for getting short yardage first downs and extra points.

My heart was not into playing football, but I stuck it out and earned my precious "big" varsity letter. Roger Clem and I recently watched a 1965 Greenon football film and it was kind of neat seeing us play back then.

My high school years were for the most part very enjoyable. There were some disconcerting events like the assassination of Malcolm X and President John F. Kennedy and the evening news reporting daily on the Vietnam War. The war seemed far away, literally over 8,000 miles, and of very little concern to us high school students.

* * *

To offset the assassination of President Kennedy, America was taken by storm by a British rock group, "The Beatles!"

I began dating classmate Peggy Shank my junior year and we shared many good times together. We doubled to the Junior Prom with Jeff Michael and Rosemary Pilcher and to the Senior Prom with Roger Clem and Peggy Meade. We attended dances and parties and many other school functions.

Peg and I doubled with Jeff and Rosemary quite a bit because Jeff lost his license trying to outrun a police car one night. We were in his '61 Ford with a 289 engine, trying to lose a police car on the back roads. When we finally stopped and pulled over, we discovered that the police car had overheated and needed water for the radiator. Jeff's home was not far from where we were stopped, so he went to get water for the policeman. No, he didn't let us off the hook.

Greenon High School was not lacking in attractive girls, as there were many. My girlfriend, Peggy, became our Greenon FFA Chapter Queen, then the Clark County FFA Queen, and then the 2nd runner-up in the State FFA Queen contest. I have always suspected that Peggy had something to do with me being elected as Greenon's 1966 Senior Class President, because she was one of the students who counted the ballots for class president for the class of 1966, but she'll never tell.

Before Peggy reigned as queen, classmate Linda Spahr was Greenon's Homecoming Queen, our Greenon FFA Chapter Queen, the County FFA Queen, the State FFA Queen and the Ohio State Fair Queen. That's a lot of queen titles! She was a very busy girl reigning as queen that year.

The Queen's Court
1965-66

Nancy Harvey

Kathy West

Sally Parks

I really liked FFA (Future Farmers of America) and was the chapter vice-president my senior year. John King, Jim Hunter, and I won a beef judging contest and had our picture in the newspaper shaking hands with some millionaire. I also got 4th place in our state land judging contest. And our Parliamentary Procedure Team won the district contest and our FFA instructor, Jim Stickley, was very proud of our chapter.

Jim Hunter, State sentinel, and John King, a member of the national FFA band, inspect the soil in one of the FFA fields.

Future Farmers of America Officers

C. Swaney; J. Hunter; S. Pencil; R. Ark; J. King; S. Waddle; J. Maurer.

My scholastic performance in high school was basically average and I was very grateful for classmate Gail Mc-Donald's help in getting me through Mr. Dubb's biology class. I laugh when I think about Fred Henry's bug collection that he submitted. His mounted bugs looked like they had been thrown around in a blender. Mr. Dubbs asked, "Fred, where did you get your collection of bugs?" and Fred replied, "From off my Dad's radiator this morning."

My other classes included Latin (Miss Estle), Algebra (Mrs. Hampshire), Chemistry (Mr. Graham), Geometry (Mr. Smith), and Vo-Ag (Mr. Stickley).

One funny thing that happened was when Roger Clem and I were in Mr. Holland's World History class. We were taking a pretty big test. Roger sat right behind me, and we decided that we'd collaborate on the test, (cheat). To our surprise, when the tests were handed back, Roger and I both scored 95% and Mr. Holland wrote "-5 for cheating." Holy Moly!

I want to mention at this juncture that my younger brother Nick and I were employed in the summer at **Spiegelmeyer Grocery Store** on Montgomery Avenue (aka Rebert Pike). We mostly ran the snack bar making hamburgers (7 for $1.00), chicken dinners, French fries, fish sandwiches, milk shakes, and ice cream cones, sundaes, etc. This little grocery store was located where State Street empties onto Montgomery Ave.

Another way that we made money in the summer was baling hay. Our family farm was next door to Art and Doris Overholser's farm and we kids baled hay and straw over there quite a bit. I believe our starting pay was $.50 /hr.

I was driving a 1957 Ford when school began in 1964. The car was half mine and half my brother Steve's. My dad bought the car from my Uncle Gordon who worked at a car dealership in Dayton, for $75.

My first car, a 1957 Ford

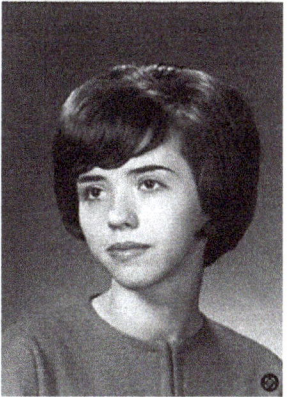

Gail McDonald

One morning, I was driving to Gail McDonald's house to pick her up for my brother, Steve, who was riding with me in the car, along with Julian (Buck) Wright. I was driving in what was then a new housing development in Enon, at the end of Rebert Pike and Enon-Xenia Rd. There were no stop signs in place yet. A Corvette suddenly t-boned the right front of my car. The impact threw me out of the car and onto the pavement and the next thing I remember is waking up in an ambulance. I think my mother rode in the ambulance with me to Mercy Hospital. My chin had a cut and needed stitches and when they finished stitching me up, I was told to get off the gurney and go home. I sat up, tried to stand up, and fell to the floor. I remained in the hospital for three days.

I only had one visitor while I was in the hospital, and God used this event to teach me a valuable lesson. My one visitor's name was Penny and she lived on Old Mill Road near Karen Woods off Rebert Pike, not far from our farm. She was a bit overweight, and pimply-faced and her family appeared to be not well off. There were kids who at times made disparaging remarks about her, belittled her, and made jokes about the way she looked.

Penny was the only classmate at Greenon who took the time to come visit me the three days I was hospitalized and to see how I was doing. I will never forget her or her thoughtfulness, and the lesson God taught me.

It happened one day after school that Roger Clem was to take me home and he was driving his brother Louis's '59 Corvette. It was the first time that I'd ever been in a car that went over 100 miles per hour. No seat belts, fiberglass body, no brains!

* * *

After graduation at 17 years of age, almost 18, I applied to attend Wright State College in the Fall. The campus only contained four buildings at that time: Allyn Hall, Oleman Hall, Millett Hall, and Fawcett. It was not yet a university, but it was growing. This college was designed to accommodate handicapped students and it had underground tunnels to each of the buildings.

For two summers while in college, I worked at Steel Products Engineering Co. and my good friend Roger Clem worked there also, as did Charlie Swaney and Jim Maurer who both worked at the Baker Road plant. I worked as a tool grinder with Bill Paxon and Bob Wagner. Bill always referred to me as "the Trainee." He was 27 years old at the time and I thought of him as old.

I'll never forget Bill. Good memories. He had a 650

Triumph Bonneville motorcycle, and it sounded so cool when he started it up. He wore a flat top haircut and rolled his cigarettes up in his short sleeve t-shirt. He reminded me of the actor Jimmy Dean.

My second summer, I worked in the tool crib with a guy who called everyone a "Fat Rat." God only knows why. At this time, I began drinking coffee with cream and sugar. I had also started smoking that summer while baling hay at Jim Hunter's father's farm. Jeff Michael offered me a Kool cigarette (my very first), and I got hooked on the menthol taste and didn't quit until boot camp in the Army. At lunch time, Roger Clem and I would park our butts on the sidewalk outside the Steel Products building and eat our packed lunch sitting on the sidewalk. We had 1/2 hour to eat.

Steel Products 1944   5+ acres   Made Bell Helicopter parts for Vietnam Huey helicopters

I began college in the fall of 1966 with strong aspirations and plans for the future, but it wasn't to be. I soon grew tired of going to school and studying for tests and being broke most of the time. My grades fell and when I was placed on probation for a trimester in November of 1967, I received a letter from Uncle Sam to report for the draft.

I took a bus to Fort Hayes, Columbus, for my physical exam. I had a cast on my right arm at the time, compliments of helping a friend load pigs one cold Saturday morning and cracking my wrist. I passed the physical, even with a cast on my arm. I asked a sergeant there, "What about this cast on my arm?" He said, "Charlie Cong will take care of that for you!" Such compassion I've rarely seen. So began my military experience.

I learned that when a person was drafted, they would only have to serve for two years, but you would have to go wherever they assigned you, no questions asked, and there were only two branches of the service that were taking draftees at the time: the Army and the Marines. This was before the lottery system was in place.

I decided to join the Army and had to do an extra year, but I would at least have a say-so as to what training I desired. I chose to be a medical corpsman. I mainly chose to join the Army because my father served in the Army in WWII, and I wanted to follow in his footsteps. I admired my father very much. I decided I wanted to be a medic because I thought that if I had to go to Vietnam, I would probably work in an air conditioned hospital with pretty nurses all around. Right!

TSGT Wilbur J. Ark WWII U.S.Army

The time arrived to head for boot camp (eight weeks of basic training). Again, I took a bus to Fort Hayes and from there to the Columbus Airport. It was to be my very first plane ride. Before I left, three Greenon classmates came to take me out for dinner and wish me well and see me off: Charles Swaney, John King, and Jim Hunter. That was very cool of them to do. I shall never forget it.

I boarded the plane, and we took off to Fort Jackson, South Carolina. We were all recruits on this plane and many of the guys were blacks and Puerto Ricans from Harlem, New York. The date was April 4th, 1968. While in the air, there was an announcement that Martin Luther King, Jr. had been assassinated. I don't remember anyone saying anything about this incident on the plane. Everyone was quiet and remained quiet.

Being a farm kid from rural Ohio, I had very little awareness about Vietnam, and even less knowledge of the war. I had no idea what a military fort looked like. My only exposure to forts was Fort Apache on the TV series, *Rin Tin Tin*. My naiveté was really kicking in.

Arriving at the Reception Station at Fort Jackson, South Carolina, we received GI buzz haircuts and every article of clothing you can imagine, OD green, of course.

Ft. Jackson, South Carolina

After we were issued all the gear we would need in our training, we all lined up outside with our duffle bags full, waiting to be ordered to do something. My name was called to step forward, as were a few others.

To my surprise, we were told that we were skipping basic training and going straight to helicopter machine gunner school. WHAT??? SKIPPING BOOT CAMP??? WHAT THE…..? MACHINE GUNNER SCHOOL???

"Hold on, Sergeant, I am an enlisted man and signed up to be a medic."

"Ok, get back in line." Whew, that was close!!

Helicopter machine gunner/door gunner

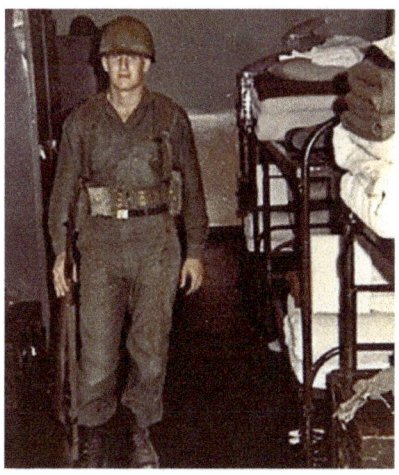

We were transported to a place dubbed "Drag Ass Hill" and assigned to an old WWII barracks. Sgt. Barnes was my drill instructor and he had been to Vietnam and was Airborne Infantry. He also had received a Purple Heart.

And he loved to run!! Well, I lost 30+ pounds after eight weeks of training.

A former Greenon classmate and good friend, Jeff Michael, had started his basic training about six weeks ahead of me. We touched base once for a short visit. He headed to Vietnam after combat engineering training. I was Jeff's best man at his wedding. Remember, Peggy and I double dated with Jeff and Rosemary Pilcher quite a bit in high school.

I made a good friend in basic training, Howard Albert. He was playing and touring with the 5th Dimension rock group and was at Caesar's Palace, Las Vegas, when he received his draft notice. We remain in touch to this day. We also trained together in AIT (Advanced Individual Training) as medics, at Fort Sam Houston, Texas, for 10 weeks.

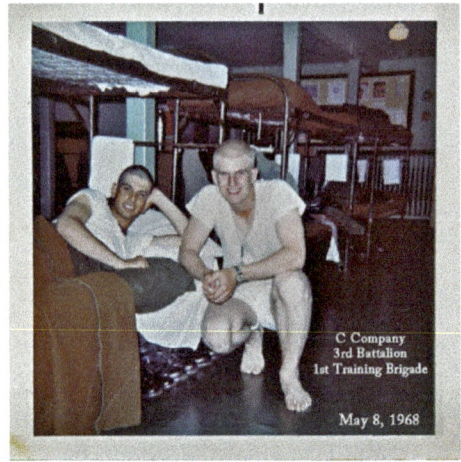 

Howard Albert

Howie and his mother. (above)

Company D, 4th Medical Battalion

We did a lot of things together: went to drag races on weekends; a Billy Graham Crusade in San Antonio; and visited the Alamo, of course, and the Air Force Academy.

There was a huge assembly at the end of our training cycle. I was surprised when they called my name to receive an award which stated that I had been selected as the "Trainee of the Cycle." That was quite a surprise.

DEPARTMENT OF THE ARMY
HEADQUARTERS U.S.ARMY MEDICAL TRAINING CENTER
FORT SAM HOUSTON, TEXAS 78234

AKPSH-T-T

16 August 1968

SUBJECT: Letter of Commendation

PVT Randall W. Ark, RA 11 838 458
Company D, 4th Battalion
U. S. Army Medical Training Center
Fort Sam Houston, Texas

1. I take this opportunity to commend you for having been selected as an Outstanding Trainee of Company D, 4th Battalion, USAMEDTC.

2. In a class of 94 trainees, you were selected by your cadre and peers as the trainee who most distinguished himself by example and service as the Outstanding Trainee of your class.

3. It is a pleasure to have personnel with your initiative, ability and interest as members of the Army Medical Service team.

CHARLES C. PIXLEY
Colonel, Medical Corps,
Commanding

At the close of our 10-week training at Ft Sam Houston, many of us received orders for Vietnam. *I needed a smoke!*

For a complete memoir of my time in Vietnam, my book mentioned above has all that information. You can order a copy anywhere books are sold.

* * *

After a year had passed in Vietnam, I bid farewell to Billy Keegan at the Chicago airport. He left for Pittsburgh, and

I headed for Springfield, landing at the Vandalia-Dayton, Ohio airport. Home, again.

My good friend whom I dated before going into the service, Cheryl England, picked me up at the Dayton Airport and we left for home. We traveled on roads that weren't there when I left for the Army.

I asked her once, years later, what was I like on the way home. She said that I was very quiet and mostly just looked out the window.

At last, I saw our little house at the end of our lane on our farm and the farmhouse down the lane where my brothers, my sister, and I were raised. I cannot describe the feeling. Two days ago, I was in Vietnam and today I am on our family's farm. I was to learn that the quick change I experienced wasn't very helpful in transitioning to civilian life.

I said goodbye to Cheryl and stood in front of the farm-house just staring, still holding my duffle bag. I walked toward the front door; it was a Sunday morning, and my family was in attendance at Rocky Point Church on Old Mill Road.

I was standing on the farmhouse front porch when I saw Dad's car raising dust, coming down the lane. He had no idea that I would be there. He stepped from his car and saw me on the front porch. He walked up the entry side-walk and wrapped his arms around me and said, "Welcome home, son." There was a letter that Dad wrote to me in Vietnam that meant so much to me when he wrote, "Don't ever feel like you are alone over there, because a part of me is there with you." I still get tears thinking about it.

It was then I saw mom's car coming and I could hear my sister screaming in joy. She was so happy I was home. It felt very good to be home and around loved ones.

My mother had saved all my letters home and banked the money I had sent home for safe keeping.

I have always found it curious that no one in my family ever asked me about my time in Vietnam. "What were my living conditions, what did I eat, what duties did I have, was I scared all the time, did I have any friends?" I suppose they figured that I didn't want to talk about it.

Fortunately, I didn't experience what many veterans did upon arriving home. There were articles in the Springfield News/Sun, however, that expressed derogatory remarks towards Vietnam veterans. I even kept an article that stated that Vietnam veterans were considered "suckers" for fighting in Vietnam.

During my 30 days at home, I attended a couple of homecoming parties, one with Greenon classmates, and another one over at my Aunt Helen's. My cousin, Bobby, Aunt Helen's son, told me that my Aunt Helen worried quite a bit about me while I was in Vietnam. I have just recently found that out. I would have never known otherwise.

Jon Allison, Roger Clem, and I took a trip to Niagara Falls just for the heck of it. Good times! They interrupted my date with Patti Ditzel in her driveway to pick me up to go.

I remember being invited over for dinner at classmates' houses and they would ask me if I wanted roast beef or chicken or steak, food like that. I told them that I'd prefer a hot dog or hamburger, and surprised, they would ask, "Are you sure?" After Vietnam, I was pretty low maintenance.

For a while, upon returning home, I found it hard to sleep. I began drinking a pint of Southern Comfort before bed every night. I turned out the lights in the farm-house bedroom upstairs and sat in the dark and drank my Southern Comfort. I forget how long this went on, but it stopped at my next duty station, Fort Carson, Colorado.

A few years ago, I was reading James Bradley's book, "Flags of our Fathers" about the battle of Iwo Jima and of his father's (John Bradley) part as one of the flag raisers on Mount Suribachi, Iwo Jima. His father was a medical corpsman.

A quote from the book, *"Flags of Our Fathers"*.

For many veterans, their memories of combat receded; supplanted by happy peacetime experiences. But there were others for whom the memories did not die, but were somehow contained. And for a few, the memories were howling demons that ruled their nights.

Among these last, a disproportionate number, I believe, are corpsmen.

It was the corpsman, after all, who saw the worst of the worst. A Marine rifleman might see his buddy shot down beside him, and regret the loss for the rest of his life. But in the moment, he kept going. That was his training, his mission.

But the corpsman saw *only* the results. His entire mission on Iwo was to hop from blown face to severed arm, doing what he could under heavy fire to minimize the damage, staunch the flow, ease the agony.

The corpsman remembered. And their memories ruled the night.

Forgetting had not come easily for John Bradley. It had taken him awhile to forget. He may have spoken about Iwo for only seven or eight disinterested minutes to Elizabeth Van Gorp on their first date. But after they were married, my mother told me, he wept at night, in his sleep. He wept in his sleep for four years.

James Bradley

Well, I packed up my things and headed to my next duty station, Fort Carson, Colorado. The year was 1969 and I was to remain there until January of 1971. I drove straight through to Colorado Springs and if I recall, I think it took 21 hours. Fort Carson is located on the outskirts of Colorado Springs. I discovered that Billy Keegan was stationed there too. I was so glad about that.

We were very close to the Rocky Mountains, especially Pike's Peak. We bunked in the barracks for a while, shared an apartment in Colorado Springs for a while, frequented the Old Corral Saloon, and became close friends with Judy Albin and her daughter Kammi.

We explored the Garden of the Gods at night, and took a trip to Provo, Utah. Billy had a big poster of The Beatles from the Abbey Road Album. It hung over his bed in the barracks.

I was stationed at Fort Carson from October 1969 to January 1971. I had many experiences while stationed in Colorado, some good, and some I'm not too proud of. I met some very nice people, though, and made some good friends.

I took pre-law classes at Colorado University and did pretty well. I also took bass guitar lessons after buying a Hofner bass guitar. I dated a teacher for a while and we went to Chihuahua, Mexico together with another couple for a few days.

My brother, Steve, drove out with his girlfriend, Meg to see me, and classmate Jay Allen came to see me, and we tooled around for a couple days up around Boulder. My first cousin, Johnny Robert Linkhart scheduled me at Wright State University so I could get a three month early out to attend college there.

College seemed easier this time around. I majored in Psychology, which was pretty much useless as far as bachelor's degrees go, but I, at least, ended with a 3.5 average, which was very good for me.

Since there were many grade school and high school teachers in my family, I decided to try that route and obtain a master's in education (MEd.) Now, education courses were relatively easy compared to Psychology and I was even asked by a math professor, Dr. Hutchcraft, if I would help him teach an Educational Statistics class at Wright State University.

The pay wasn't much, but the experience had value. I taught for two quarters. Dr. Hutchcraft was a good guy. He told me that he was going to move to Florida and teach high school math and would not tell anyone that he had a doctorate degree in math. He said teaching high school was much more fun than college.

I ended grad school with a 4.0 average and applied for a teaching position at Town and Country School on Van Buren Avenue in Springfield, off Burnett Road. My graduate degree was in Special Education because that was the fastest way for me to get into the field of education. I was hired and began teaching in January of 1976. I obtained a permanent certificate later on after taking additional courses.

The students attending there were a mix of Down's Syndrome kids, multi-handicapped, and moderate and profoundly retarded kids. The principal at that time was Mr. Joe Horner, who was a very nice man. I was assigned an assistant, Violet Lawson, and we worked together a few years at Town and Country. I had continued playing in a country band I was in at the time for extra money while teaching, as I was only making $125/week.

Sometimes I would be out until 3:00 a.m. playing and be dead tired the next day at school. One time my principal, Joe Horner, was escorting a visitor around our school and when they came into my room, I had my head down on my desk, fast asleep. To say I was embarrassed is an understatement. I realized then, my burning the candle at both ends wasn't working, so I had to quit playing, at least through the week.

I need to back up a little now. In the fall of 1967, as I related previously, I was placed on probation at WSU and was drafted into the military. My first summer at home, 1969, out of the Army, I obtained a job as a youth counselor for inner city youth and drove a bus for disadvantaged kids to different places, parks and such.

I played bass guitar in my first rock band called PRESSURE. It was a three-piece band starting out, with my brother Bruce on drums and Chuck Zoubek on lead guitar. Later on, Bill Udderback joined the group with his Hammond B-3 organ and upright Leslie speaker. We played quite a bit at the Co-Ho Club just outside of Enon. One time a big fight was started while we were playing Soul Sacrifice by Santana. Roger and Peggy Clem were there, John King was there, and I forget who else. Chuck, our band's lead guitarist, met his future wife, Brenda, there.

Over the next few years I played in various bands, some as a bass player and some as a lead and rhythm guitarist. In 1974, I met my future wife, Sharon K. Cutlip, on a blind date. It was Chuck's girlfriend, Brenda, who fixed us up. I found out later that Sharon's mother, Maggie Eileen Looney and her father, William Eldon Cutlip, also met on a blind date, as did my mother and father.

Sharon was seven years younger than I was, but we seemed pretty compatible. We will have been married for 50 years come March 22. My best man was Charles D. Swaney, and the groomsmen were Roger Clem, Jim Knotts, Dennis Turner, and Chuck Zoubek. I will be writing more about Sharon later on.

With the help of Junior Smith serving as my sound engineer and Sound Space Labs in Yellow Springs, we produced my first, and only, Christian album on cassette and later on CD, "Living By the Book."

It received airplay on three radio stations, but WEEC gave it the most airtime. I can't describe the feeling I had hearing it for the first time, one of my songs being played on the car radio while driving home from somewhere. Also, a nice article was written in the newspaper about my going from country rock to gospel music.

Randy Ark

Living By The Book

Randy Ark - Living By The Book

1. Livin' By The Book
2. The Minor Prophets
3. Bystanders Lament
4. You Don't Know
   Where You're Goin'
5. Samson
6. There's Just One Way
7. With All Your Heart
8. When You Call His Name
9. Jesus My Friend
10. Part-Time Believer
11. The Stranger

All the songs were written by Randy Ark except "Samson", written by Terry Gilkyson ©1959.

All selections were produced and arranged by Randy Ark and Junior Smith at Creation Lab. All selections mastered and copied at Soundspace Studios, Yellow Springs, Ohio. All selections but Samson" are copyrighted 1992-1993 ©.

Many thanks to Bruce Ark on drums, Chuck Beck on guitar and Dean Hoke, Sheila Cutlip & Barb Stigers on Vocals.

The cover design and illustration is by Debbie Kelly and Kara Ark.

A special thank-you to my engineer, Junior Smith. His friendship, encouragement and love of our Lord Jesus has been a blessing to me and to this production.

I am blessed beyond measure and marvel at His grace. I thank Jesus for allowing me to serve Him in this way. A special thanks to Pastor Marv Wiseman, Paul Pontis, and the many people of Grace Bible Church for their support and help. And to my family and my wife for their encouragement and patience.

I pray these songs will be honoring unto the Lord and an encouragement to believers.
For additional information contact: Grace Bible Church, 1500 Groop Road, Springfield, Ohio 45504

Sharon and I had three children: Nathan Randall Ark (1981), Kara Eileen Ark (1982), and Matthew David Ark (1986). I love each of my children dearly and am very proud of them.

After nine years teaching at Town and Country School, I secured a job at South Vienna Middle School, 7th and 8th grade Special Education. Larry Shaffer was the principal there and Jeff Binz was the vice-principal. Both are now deceased. My first room was a converted hallway, but we made do.

The Northeastern School District superintendent was Carl Frasure, a Korean War veteran, also a medic, I believe.

I taught at South Vienna Middle School for 24 years and I bought three years of Army time so I could retire at the 36 year rate. The effects of Agent Orange were taking its toll on me, and I could not move as handily as I used to, so retirement happened at the right time.

During my time at South Vienna, I had an assistant for a couple of years, Martha Tackett, whose husband, Roger Tackett, was a County Commissioner and was paralyzed from the waist down from a sniper's bullet in Vietnam, 1967. Roger and I have become good friends. We are in the same Purple Heart Chapter 620.

At South Vienna, I was no longer labeled a *Special Ed. teacher*, but now I was an *"Inclusion Specialist."* Sounds important, doesn't it? I made some good friends while teaching there and had many positive experiences with fellow teachers, students' parents, and participating in extra-curricular activities.

I was in charge of setting up our school's sound system for programs, assemblies, basketball games, and school dances. I felt that I had many friends there. My kids … Nathan, Kara, and Matthew, rode to school with me each morning. When any of my kids were involved in sports (football, basketball, track, or tennis) I felt like an Uber Driver.

Sharon wanted to try working at the Honda Plant and she did so for a few years and enjoyed it. Her mother, Maggie Eileen, came to live with us for a while until we could no longer care for her, and we had to place her at Oakwood Village. Sharon's parents were lovely people, and we shared many good times with them.

After retirement, I became more and more involved with veterans and veteran's activities. I had, and still have, a great desire to assist veterans in getting information to them, making sure that each veteran is aware of all the entitlements they've earned by serving their country. Many veterans are not aware of the services that are afforded to them at the Veterans Clinic and Veterans Commission for example.

I started on my path to helping veterans thanks to Martha Tackett. Upon learning that I had developed Type II Diabetes, she suggested I get assigned a doctor at the Veterans Clinic. That's when I met Earl Morse, the co-founder of the *Honor Flight Network*.

There was another project I took on and it was to create a history of Springfield on DVD's. I spent seven years researching on this project and came away with a two DVD history.

There are two WWII veterans I want to mention whom I became very close to: John Kunkel and Harold Deane. Both were in the thick of the fighting in WWII, and both were wounded. John fought in the Battle of the Hurtgen Forest and the Battle of the Bulge, serving in the 4th Infantry Division. Harold made six beach landings with the 3rd Infantry Division, beginning in 1942 in North Africa, then two landings in Sicily, two in Italy, and one in southern France. Harold was away from home for three years and three months. I became like a son to him and his wife, Betty. I was asked to give the eulogy at his funeral. I did so, with honor.

Another veteran who has been instrumental in my life is Earl Morse. He and Jeff Miller, together, founded the Honor Flight Network. In 2005, Earl began transporting WWII veterans in private planes from the Springfield Airport. He arranged for six private planes carrying twelve WWII veterans to fly to Washington D.C. to see their memorial. No veteran who has gone on an Honor Flight trip has ever had to pay a penny.

As of today, there are hubs all over America and many thousands of veterans have gone. Now, Earl was a PA at the veterans' clinic located on Burnett Rd. at the time and I was assigned to be under his care. He was very, very, good and he helped me to get disability compensation from the VA. I eventually was categorized as 100% disabled.

*Honor Flight
Co-Founder
Earl Morse*

I got a call one night from Earl who was at a National Honor Flight Board of Directors meeting, and he said the board voted they wanted me to be on the National Board of Directors for the Honor Flight Network. I accepted and served on the board for five years.

I took an Honor Flight trip myself and met Sen. Bob Dole with the help from fellow Vietnam veteran, Alan Bailey who works with the Dayton hub. He arranged for me and five other Purple Heart members to go together. My son Matthew was my designated guardian, and he did a wonderful job. To experience that with him was so special. I forgot to mention that one time our board was asked to assist the History Channel Network in bringing veterans from all over the United States to the Vietnam Wall for a ceremony. It was that day that I met Joe Galloway who authored "We Were Soldiers Once, and Young." I was honored to meet him.

Below: We veterans were greeted by a throng of people at the Dayton International Airport in Vandalia.

I just remembered that when Sharon and I were at a veteran's event in Columbus once, I got to meet and shake hands with Newt Gingrich and Ollie North. Pretty cool, I thought.

Meeting Newt Gingrich and Ollie North in Columbus, Ohio

The members of Chapter 620, Military Order of the Purple Heart (M.O.P.H.) encouraged me to keep trying to get documentation for my Purple Heart medal that I had never received. Congressman Warren Davidson helped to push my papers through to a military board and I waited, hoping for acclimation.

After a total of 16 years, I was alone at home one day and the doorbell rang. I answered the door and there was a UPS driver standing there, who handed me a small package all wrapped up tightly. I thanked him and saw that the package was for me. I went back into my office and unwrapped my personalized Purple Heart medal. My name is even inscribed on the back of the medal. I cannot describe the feelings and emotions I had at that moment. I could now have a vote in the MOPH meetings or hold office. It wasn't long before I was voted Commander of Chapter 620, MOPH.

I had mentioned before that I was involved in treating wounded under an intense barrage of rockets and mortars. I received my third Army Commendation Medal, but with a "V" device. Because of this medal, years later, I was inducted into the Ohio Military Hall of Fame for Valor. This was in 2015, as I recall. There was huge ceremony at the Statehouse in Columbus, Ohio. My whole family was there and some close friends, Charles Swaney, Doug Wood, and Gary Sellers. It was quite an honor to be seated on stage with other medal recipients.

Ohio Military Hall of Fame for Valor
Columbus, Ohio 4/24/15

Also, earlier that same year, I was honored to be inducted into the Greenon High School Hall of Fame, along with classmate Micheal Lambert, and Enon Mayor, Elmer Beard. We were honored because of our community and military contributions after graduation. It was nice to be honored at my alma mater.

I was the keynote speaker there when the first Greenon Memorial was dedicated to honor classmates Billy Bloomfield, Clyde Saunders, David Dye, and Willard DeLong, Jr., who lost their lives in the Vietnam War.

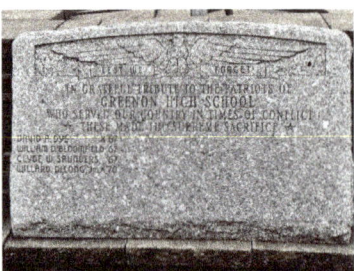

When I first became a member of Chapter 620, Military Order of the Purple Heart (M.O.P.H.), the members were in the process of getting donations for a War Dog Memorial that would be placed in Clark County's Veterans Memorial Park. This is the first of five memorials I was to be involved in procuring for our Clark County Veterans

Memorial Park. This memorial was dedicated in 2011 to acknowledge and honor war dogs and their trainers.

The Penda Publishing Company *Since 1994*

Local War Dog Memorial Gets Listed At The Smithsonian Institute

Mayor Warren R. Copeland and Purple Heart Commander David A. Bauer. Photo by Randall W. Ark.

In 2013, I was approached by Doug Wood and Dave Bauer to help them with another project of sub-naming Fountain Ave, Purple Heart Way. My lawyer and childhood best friend, Charles Swaney, had his law office along Fountain Ave. so he had secretary type up the names of all the residents that would be affected by our "Purple Heart Way" sign who resided along Fountain Ave.

Petitions needed to be signed, and permissions granted from various organizations. I presented our idea to the Springfield City Commission on three different occasions.

The Commission finally agreed to pay half the cost of our signs if our Chapter 620 MOPH came up with the other half. As we left the City Commission meeting, one of the commissioners yelled, "Randy, you better come up with your half!" I yelled back, "I'm betting that we'll have our half before you do!" And we did! Two of the signs located where Fountain Ave. crosses Main Street and High Street were backlit at night. I really like those.

Purple Heart Way signs installed on Fountain Ave. from High Street to McCreight Ave.

The first Purple Heart Way sign goes up on Feb. 22, 2012

It was in May of 2015 that I was contacted by the Springfield Foundation and a lawyer representing an elderly lady from Enon, Ohio. This lady's husband flew B-26's on D-Day and she had been following my activities in the Clark County Veterans Memorial Park and she wished to donate money to assist me in my efforts. The amount was enough to create an endowment at the Springfield Foundation. The money was designated for the upkeep of the veterans' park area. I was so pleased that somebody was paying attention to what we were doing in the park, and especially pleased to be gifted that donation.

Also, in 2015, Dave Bauer and I dedicated another memorial in Veterans Park that we called, The Dog Tag Memorial. With assistance from Josh Walters at Dodds Memorials, we came away with a design that we were pleased with. The memorial would be in the shape of a dog tag and would have the names of every person from Clark County that perished in the Vietnam War. I wanted to add a "Soldiers Cross" to be placed next to the Dog Tag, so that happened.

During the planning stages for this memorial, Dave became the State Purple Heart Commander for the State of Ohio, so he wasn't around too much, which left the workload on me.

Regardless, on September 26, 2015, we dedicated our "Dog Tag Memorial" at the Clark County Veterans Memorial Park. There was a large gathering at this ceremony. This memorial served as closure for many folks. There are 63 names on this memorial. County Commissioner Rick Lohnes was our keynote speaker for this event, and I spoke also. This memorial proved to be a very necessary memorial for all those who had known these men whose names were inscribed on our granite dog tag.

MILITARY CLARK COUNTY

Veterans set out to erect local Vietnam memorial

Springfield tribute would require $12,500 to fund, organizers say.

By Andrew McGinn
Staff Writer

SPRINGFIELD — In Randy Ark's mind, Billy Bloomfield will always be an athletic kid with a bright and flat top.

He never saw Bloomfield any other way - the Greenon High School graduate was killed serving with the Marines on June 2, 1969, in Vietnam's Quang Nam Province.

Ark was in Vietnam himself at the time.

For Dave Bauer, the death is Leon Doug Provitor of his cousin, Northwestern graduate Floyd Skaggs, became the sole reason for existence in 1968.

Bauer and Ark both survived the Vietnam War, and they now want to fund and build a permanent memorial to the 62 young men from Clark County who didn't.

"There's survivor's guilt," Ark, 64, explained recently. "Time and I have always felt we need to speak and represent and keep alive the twenty one that were lost.

"We have the opportunity," he added, "they don't. We're doing it for our friends who can't do it."

The two local Vietnam veterans are setting out to raise $12,500 needed to erect a granite monument in the shape of a giant dog tag that will be inscribed with the 62 names.

To donate, contact Ark by email at randy.ark48@gmail.com or call him at 937-206-0959.

They want to place the monument in Veterans Park, near a ...

Memorial continues on C3

Mike Spradlin from Spradlin Bros. Welding Company volunteered to create a chain for the Dog Tag Memorial. This normally would have cost around $3000, but Mike said this was his way of donating to the memorial. Mike is, and has always been, a staunch supporter of veterans and especially Chapter 620's projects.

I really appreciate this picture which demonstrates the effect our Dog Tag Memorial had on some of those folks who attended our dedication at the Clark County Veterans Memorial Park, in September of 2015

Dedication of Dog Tag Memorial

On July 3, 2016 another memorial was dedicated in Clark County's Veterans Memorial Park to the men of the 1st Battalion, 3rd Marine Regiment, 1964-1965, in honor of their service and sacrifices in the Republic of Vietnam. The men who the monument was dedicated for were the first Marine boots on the ground in Da Nang, Vietnam, 1965.

While working to dedicate the Dog Tag Memorial, I couldn't help but notice a small memorial that resembled a grave marker situated under a tree close to where our Dog Tag monument was located. It was always decorated with flags and flowers and was inscribed, 1st Battalion, 3rd Marine Regiment. I later found out that it had been placed there in 1988 and was cared for by the Ladies Auxiliary of the Springfield Marine Corps League. It wasn't long after our Dog Tag dedication that I was summoned to meet with some Marines at the Veterans Memorial Park. These Marines asked me if I would assist them in getting a larger memorial for the men who were honored on the small one. I agreed to help them. After a few meetings with Josh Walters at Dodds Memorials, we came up with a design that we were all comfortable with.

One of the Marines, Roger Warren, provided me with some photographs of when they were in Vietnam in 1965, and we had them lasered onto the face of the memorial. We placed the smaller memorial at the foot of the larger one. There were Marines from all different parts of the United States attending our dedication of this memorial, and there were many tears and thanks.

Dedication of Marine Memorial

Honoring two Marine veterans from Springfield

First Marine boots on the ground on Nov. 9 1965. Da Nang, Vietnam.

Roger Warren USMC

Dewey Miller USMC

Assistant Director Brad Boyer at National Trail Parks and Recreation District asked if I might consider helping to raise money to renovate the Veterans Park. Marine Ronnie Coss and I met with Brad and a professional landscaping lady from Columbus and put together a design for a renovated Veterans Park. This new design required that my memorials be moved from their current location to a new area along Buck Creek. I resisted at first but finally went along with the proposal. Currently, there are three memorials, two memorial benches, and three military flags located in our "Vietnam Area of Veteran Park."

Clark County Veterans Memorial Park
August 12, 2020

Another endeavor I took upon myself was to create military street banners on my computer and have Mac-Ray's create the banners that were to hang along the bridge on Fountain Avenue and along Cliff Park Road that runs through Veterans Park.

In 2018, on November 10, I was asked to be the keynote speaker at the 243rd Marine Birthday Ball that was held in the upper level of the VFW Post #1031. I was honored to be asked.

Dr. Ski Schanher served on the Ferncliff Cemetery Board, and he asked me if I would help him in placing memorials in Ferncliff Cemetery and Arboretum. These memorials will be dedicated to every war where Clark County residents participated. Each memorial will contain a description of that particular war and when it occurred. Dr. Schanher asked if I might do an inscription about the War on Terror. With the help of my brother, Steve, we created an inscription that is used for that memorial.

I did not receive authorization papers for my Purple Heart medal until January 11, 2021. A UPS truck stopped by our house and handed me a small package. I opened the package, thinking that it was medication from the VA, and discovered my long-awaited Purple Heart Medal. Thanks to the efforts of Representative Warren Davidson, I finally had my medal. It had been 16 years since I first applied for the papers to verify my Purple Heart and 55 years since I had been wounded. It was shortly after that, I was elected to be the Commander of Springfield's Chapter 620, Military Order of the Purple Heart. We are down to just five members now.

My most current project involved Greenon High School, my high school alma mater. As I mentioned before, a few years ago I was asked to be the keynote speaker at Greenon High School to commemorate Veterans Day. Also, at that time, a memorial was being dedicated to four Greenon students who had served and died in the Vietnam War. These students' names were William D. Bloomfield '67, David A. Dye '67, Clyde W. Saunders, '67, and Willard DeLong, Jr. '70.

The years passed and the effects of the weather took its toll on that memorial dedicated back then. And through a series of events and meetings, it was decided to level Greenon High school that had been in use since 1955 and to build a new Greenon Campus in Enon on the corner of Rebert Pike and Enon-Xenia Rd.

My initial plan was to create a new memorial and have it made and placed at the new school. But I was convinced by others that the old memorial area would be a better placement, because former students would know where that area was and more people would be able to see it, so it was decided to preserve and renovate the existing memorial area that was already in place along Tecumseh Road.

In the interim of having the new memorial created at Dodds Memorials in Xenia, it came to my attention there were others who wanted to be a part of this endeavor. At the Enon-Greenon Alumni Banquet last year, I was seated next to Superintendent Darrin Knapke. We spoke at length about the old memorial area along Tecumseh Road. He was very supportive of a renovation project and took an active role in helping get this done. So, Superintendent Darrin Knapke, Dennis Henry, Brenda Pyles Sweet, Dennis Brown, Josh Walters from Dodds Memorials, and yours truly began planning what we would like to see done and what steps we should take first.

The Greenon Class of 1969 provided a new center flagpole. We contacted Jesse Ward of New *View Property Maintenance and Hardscapes.* His company removed all existing shrubbery and planted new shrubbery and put down fresh mulch. The pavers and benches were power washed, and all outlying memorials were relocated into the newly renovated area. The folks from Dodds Memorials came one day and dug the footers and poured the cement used to support two different memorials.

On November 10, 2023 the Greenon Memorial Area was dedicated. The memorials and monuments that were scattered around on the Greenon property were collected and placed into the new area. A QR code was placed onto the newest memorial, and the names and pictures of every veteran who served in the military from the Enon-Greenon area would be placed on the QR code and be available for anyone to scan. It took a few months to do this.

Another project was completed before this one. I forget how it started, but here's how it all went down.

Brenda Sweet (from the Enon Community Historical Society) and I took it upon ourselves to create a power point of pictures of every senior class in the Enon-Greenon area for every year that was available. Brenda had access to many of the yearbooks we needed, and she and Jennifer

Brown went about trying to get ahold of the yearbooks we didn't have. I did all the scanning and creating the power point. It took about three months to accomplish this.

Our power point begins in 1915 and continues to 2022. There are a few missing years, but very few. These senior class pictures are presented and displayed on a large high-definition screen placed on a wall in an area used for study hall and whatever. All a person has to do is touch the year they want to see on the screen, and it goes there. I don't know of any other school that has done this.

My brother Nick and I put together a power point to be viewed at our yearly Greenon Alumni Banquet. This power point displays the names, pictures, and military information of every student who ever attended school in our district. If you served in any capacity in our country's military, you would be acknowledged on that video for all to see.

I retired from teaching on the 23rd of October, 2007. I had taught a total of 33 years, and I bought three years of my Army time from the sick days I had accrued over the years, so I could get the most retirement money for Sharon and me. 89% is what I am getting, I believe.

My firstborn son was Nathan who arrived on a Friday the 13th in 1981, but an emergency cesarean was required to get him out. I was told that his umbilical cord was wrapped around his neck, but doctors Billing and Figge got him out okay.

I had watched on TV many times the behaviors of expectant fathers in a waiting room, pacing back and forth and smoking cigarettes. So that's what I did. We were allowed to back then in 1981. When the nurse brought Nathan in for the first time, I held him, and I experienced a special bond that I have never forgotten.

Nathan has grown to be a good man whom I respect and am very proud of. He and his wife Nichole just had their first child together, Baron, in March. Nathan had another child, Morgan, from his first marriage. Morgan is a very sweet girl, and smart, too, and everyone in our families get along fine, thankfully.

Nathan played football and basketball at South Vienna Junior High, but his more adaptable sport was tennis. Nathan takes his Christian beliefs very seriously and at times our whole family attends church together. Pretty unusual these days, I think.

P.S. Nathan has his master's degree in special education and currently teaches at Fairborn Middle School in Fairborn, Ohio. I am very proud of him. He started a Bible study class at the school which is going very well. Nathan's wife, Nichole, teaches music at Mechanicsburg High school. She is fun to be around and very dedicated to her profession and she's a good mother to both Morgan and Baron.

Kara was born in 1982. She was the cutest little child I have ever seen, and I know I'm prejudiced, but she really was very cute. She had a little sassy side, too. She would sometimes discipline Nathan, and Sharon and I would laugh. She carried her care of Nathan into high school and poor Nathan couldn't get away with anything.

Kara was a very conservative straight shooter, and this persona left her feeling very much left out of things occasionally, especially with school dances. There were a few times I would be sitting on her bed with Kara in tears and I would talk with her about how God was possibly sparing herself from heartache and pain and that He would provide a suitable mate for her when the time is right. Kara was fortunate to have some very nice friends to run around with. There were times when they would all come over to our house and they would sit around our dining room table and chat and laugh.

Kara was active in our Vineyard Church youth group and one time went to Mexico on a mission trip. I remember Sharon's mother, Maggie Eileen, was in tears when Kara left on the bus. She may have thought that Kara wasn't coming back.

Kara played tennis, too, and was in a play in high school where she played Auntie Em. She enjoyed that and we enjoyed watching her.

She met and fell in love with and married Billy Thomas who is now a Wittenberg Policeman. They have twin boys who are the apples of our eyes! Those little guys are so special!! Joel and Gabriel.

Kara also has a master's degree in art education and is currently teaching art at the new Kenton Ridge High School. She is a very gifted artist. Her students think a lot of her. We are pretty proud of her, too.

Matthew was born in July, 1986. He was a natural athlete and participated in football, basketball, baseball, track, and tennis. He also loves to play golf and still does so when he can.

In high school, Matthew had special friends whom he ran around with and sometimes after a night's running around, they occasionally would all end up in my office at home and we would just sit around and talk about life and what was going on in their lives. It was a real special time for all of us. It was a time to get things off your chest, seek advice, and just share your life.

Matthew works at a Honda plant in East Liberty and lives with Sharon and me here in Northridge in our house on Bonita Avenue. He helps around here in many ways with chores, etc., and is good company for both of us. I seem to have more and more need of assistance these days, and Matthew watches me closely when we travel. I have diabetic neuropathy and all kinds of stuff due to old age and Agent Orange that was used as a defoliant to kill vegetation in Vietnam. Its effects are many and varied.

I cannot believe I am 76 years old. We appreciate that Matthew has remained here to help us out. Another plus is that Matthew and I share an interest in history, especially military history. He has accompanied me on many occasions (i.e. my Honor Flight Trip) and to hear speakers talk about their experiences in war or a topic they have studied as an expert, etc.

Sharon and I met on a blind date, as did her parents and my parents also! Sharon was 19 years old and very pretty. She had blue eyes and long blond hair and was seven years younger than me. Her family were strong Christians and attended Southgate Baptist Church on the south end of town. Pastor Joseph Stoll was the minister there.

At the time, I had been involved in various cults and Astara was my cult of choice when I first met Sharon in 1974. It was also 1974 when I completed my courses at Wright State University and had earned my Bachelor of Arts degree, majoring in Psychology. I was disappointed that Sharon could not attend my graduation ceremony.

I found out very soon that I could do nothing with a BA in Psychology, so I looked into obtaining a master's degree in something. There were many teachers in my family sphere, and I discovered that my shortest route to getting a master's degree was in Special Education, so I obtained a master's degree in education in 1977, the same year my Grandma Shump died.

An interesting side note: I performed so well in my Educational Statistics class that Dr. Hutchcraft asked me to teach a couple of quarters as his assistant, which I did. I forget what the pay was. Dr. Hutchcraft said he was going to retire and move to Florida and teach high school math and not tell anyone that he had his doctorate in math. He said that teaching high school math would be a lot more fun.

I was still employed at Rike's at the Upper Valley Mall as a weekend supervisor in "housekeeping" and I started teaching in January of 1976 at Town and Country School on Van Buren Avenue At Rike's, I made some good friends: Craig Fogle, Dennis Turner, Robert Soles, and Forest Swyers. Walter Refore was my supervisor, and a Korean War veteran.

The first band I was a member of was called "Pressure." It was my brother Bruce on drums, Chuck Zoubek on rhythm and lead guitar, and me on bass guitar. We played at many venues and had a nice repertoire of songs. The types of songs that we did had the bass following the lead riffs which helped me later on when I switched to lead guitar. Other groups I played in were called "Sundown" and "Rainbow Ridge Band."

Dennis Turner, Craig Fogle, Randy Ark, Doug White

Sharon and I lived in the Northridge Apartments (1587 Regent Street) when we were first married in March (22) of 1975 and then about a year later, we moved into a house on 2032 Westboro Ave. in Northern Estates. This house was purchased for $25,000. My foreman at Rike's Department Store, Walter Refore, occupied this house previously.

Nathan and Kara had lived in this house on Westboro Avenue, but Matthew never had. He came along when we had moved into a newer house on 5534 Ridgewood Road. West, a house that at one time belonged to Sheriff Gene Kelly, who is now a very good friend of mine, and we attend the same church, The Bridge Church.

Matthew was born while living in this house in July of 1986. Next, we moved into a new house we had built in a newly developed area in Northridge at 1307 Northfield Court (still in Northridge). We had a beautiful deck, a large swimming pool, and a big back yard.

And lastly, our house here at 1412 Bonita Avenue, is our most recent home, also here in Northridge, of course. This was in 2002. This house was once occupied by our good friends, John and Marshell Neidhart. I might add that I had never stepped foot in Northridge until I met Sharon.

I began teaching at South Vienna School in 1986. I had a little office to work from and soon became attached to certain students who were seen as troublemakers, but somehow felt comfortable talking to me about their home life, etc.

The school was beginning to incorporate "inclusion classes" into the system, so I spent less time handling a self-contained classroom and more time in regular classrooms.

I fixed up my little office with blacklight posters and a blacklight in the restroom part of my office. I posted the

Ten Commandments outside my office in the main hallway, written in Hebrew, so no one could be offended because they couldn't read Hebrew.

I became friends with a janitor there, Denny Holloway, who fought in Vietnam and was stabbed several times during a skirmish with a VC. There were very many good teachers and administrators working at South Vienna, and I felt very blessed to be in this environment.

Nathan, Kara, and Matthew all attended South Vienna School, first grade through eighth grade. They all rode to school with me every morning.

At this writing, South Vienna School no longer exists and Northeastern High School and Elementary has been erected and now occupies and is in use in that same area.

I became more and more familiar with computers at school, mainly from doing IEP's (Individual Educational Plans). For a couple of years, I was assigned an assistant, Martha Tackett. Her husband, Roger, a Marine, was wounded in Vietnam by a sniper's bullet in 1967, and became paralyzed from the waist down. Roger and I became good friends and have remained friends for many years. He served our community for several years as a County Commissioner. We now are members of the same Purple Heart Chapter 620 here in Springfield.

When it was discovered that I had Type II diabetes, Martha said I should take advantage of the VA Clinic on Burnett Road and gave me some information about a defoliant used in Vietnam called Agent Orange, a substance known to be a causative agent for Type II diabetes and other maladies. I was soon being treated at the Community Based Veterans Clinic and started to become more and more involved with the affairs of veterans.

After thirty-two years of teaching, I had not used much of my sick time and had accrued over $20,000 so I decided to buy my remaining three years of Army time so I could retire in 2007, Oct. 23rd and still receive the highest % of retirement. Was I glad? You bet I was! I miss interacting with the students, but not the regimen.

Ok, so I'm retired! Now what? I am 76 years old; Nathan is 43, Kara is 42 and Matthew is 38, and Sharon, well, never-mind...

www.ingramcontent.com/pod-product-compliance
Lightning Source LLC
Chambersburg PA
CBHW051318120626
46547CB00015B/2291